PRINCEWILL LAGANG

The Journey to Forever: A Christian Marriage Roadmap

First published by PRINCEWILL LAGANG 2023

Copyright © 2023 by Princewill Lagang

All rights reserved. No part of this publication may be reproduced, stored or transmitted in any form or by any means, electronic, mechanical, photocopying, recording, scanning, or otherwise without written permission from the publisher. It is illegal to copy this book, post it to a website, or distribute it by any other means without permission.

Princewill Lagang asserts the moral right to be identified as the author of this work.

First edition

This book was professionally typeset on Reedsy.
Find out more at reedsy.com

Contents

1	The Foundation of Love	1
2	Building the Pillars of Trust	4
3	Cultivating Compassion and Kindness	7
4	Cherishing Unity and Oneness	10
5	Nurturing Intimacy and Connection	13
6	Sustaining Hope and Resilience	16
7	Embracing Change and Growth	19
8	Fostering Family and Legacy	22
9	Sustaining Gratitude and Joy	25
10	Leaving a Legacy of Love	28
11	Celebrating the Journey	31
12	The Everlasting Covenant	34

1

The Foundation of Love

The Journey to Forever: A Christian Marriage Roadmap

In a quaint little church nestled amidst the rolling hills of a picturesque countryside, the sun's golden rays cast a warm, inviting glow upon the rustic wooden pews. A soft hymn filled the air as family and friends gathered to witness the union of two souls, joining hands in a sacred covenant. Their love story was about to unfold, written in the language of faith, hope, and devotion, on a journey to forever.

As we embark on the path of the Christian marriage roadmap, let us begin by exploring the foundational elements of love. For love is the bedrock upon which your journey is built, and understanding its significance in a Christian marriage is paramount.

1.1 The Origin of Love

"Beloved, let us love one another, for love is from God, and whoever loves has been born of God and knows God." - 1 John 4:7

Love, as the Apostle John penned, originates from the very heart of God. It is a divine gift, bestowed upon us, created in His image. Your love for one another is a reflection of God's love for His creation. As you embark on this journey together, remember that the source of your love is divine, and it carries a sacred purpose.

1.2 Love as a Choice

"In the same way, husbands should love their wives as they love their own bodies. He who loves his wife loves himself." - Ephesians 5:28

Love in a Christian marriage isn't solely a fleeting emotion but a daily choice. It's a commitment to cherish, protect, and uplift each other, just as Christ loves His church. This love transcends the temporary, and it requires unwavering dedication and selflessness.

1.3 A Threefold Cord

"Though one may be overpowered, two can defend themselves. A cord of three strands is not quickly broken." - Ecclesiastes 4:12

In a Christian marriage, love isn't a bond between two individuals alone. It's a sacred union with God at its core. Your journey to forever is a threefold cord: husband, wife, and God. By nurturing your personal relationship with Him, you strengthen the foundation of your marriage, making it resilient and unbreakable.

1.4 Forgiveness and Grace

"Be kind and compassionate to one another, forgiving each other, just as in Christ God forgave you." - Ephesians 4:32

THE FOUNDATION OF LOVE

Marriage is a journey of two imperfect individuals learning to love and forgive one another just as Christ forgave us. In your moments of imperfection, remember to extend grace and forgiveness, knowing that you, too, are forgiven. For it is in forgiveness and grace that love flourishes.

1.5 Unconditional Love

"But God commendeth his love toward us, in that, while we were yet sinners, Christ died for us." - Romans 5:8

Christian love is unconditional. Just as Christ's love for us is unwavering, let your love be steadfast, even in the face of trials and tribulations. In your commitment to each other, find the strength to love without conditions, as Christ loves you despite your shortcomings.

With these foundational elements in mind, you stand at the threshold of your Christian marriage journey. Your love story, written in the language of faith, hope, and devotion, is about to unfold. As you continue to read the chapters of your life together, remember that the journey to forever is a path illuminated by the love of God, a love that will guide you through the joys and challenges of your Christian marriage.

2

Building the Pillars of Trust

The Journey to Forever: A Christian Marriage Roadmap

In the heart of every successful Christian marriage, trust stands tall as one of the foundational pillars. Like the enduring oak tree, its roots run deep and provide stability to weather the storms of life. In this chapter, we will explore the significance of trust and how to build and nurture it in your marriage.

2.1 The Covenant of Trust

Trust is the cornerstone of any healthy and enduring marriage. It's the unwavering belief that your partner is reliable, faithful, and committed to the vows you've made before God and your loved ones. Just as God is faithful to His promises, your commitment to trust each other reflects your faith in God's guidance.

2.2 Transparency and Openness

"Whoever walks in integrity walks securely, but whoever takes crooked paths will be found out." - Proverbs 10:9

A strong foundation of trust is built on transparency and openness. It is the act of sharing your thoughts, fears, and dreams with each other. Transparency ensures that there are no hidden agendas or secrets between you, fostering an environment of honesty and safety in which trust can thrive.

2.3 Forgiving and Forgetting

"Put on then, as God's chosen ones, holy and beloved, compassionate hearts, kindness, humility, meekness, and patience, bearing with one another and, if one has a complaint against another, forgiving each other; as the Lord has forgiven you, so you also must forgive." - Colossians 3:12-13

In the journey to forever, forgiveness plays a vital role. Just as Christ forgave us, spouses should forgive one another's shortcomings and mistakes. Forgiveness allows trust to be rebuilt when it's tested and reaffirms the commitment to moving forward together with a clean slate.

2.4 Honoring Commitments

"Let your yes be yes and your no be no." - Matthew 5:37

Keeping commitments, no matter how small they may seem, is a demonstration of trustworthiness. When you fulfill promises to one another, whether it's as simple as taking out the trash or as profound as staying faithful in marriage, you are affirming your commitment and strengthening the trust between you.

2.5 Building Trust with God

"Trust in the Lord with all your heart, and do not lean on your understanding."
- Proverbs 3:5

The trust between you and your spouse is inseparable from your trust in God. By nurturing your personal relationship with Him, you gain the strength and wisdom to build and maintain trust in your marriage. Lean on His guidance and wisdom to navigate challenges and deepen your trust in each other.

2.6 Communication and Empathy

"Know this, my beloved brothers: let every person be quick to hear, slow to speak, slow to anger." - James 1:19

Effective communication and empathy are essential in building trust. Listen to your spouse with an open heart, seek to understand their perspective, and respond with kindness. A willingness to empathize fosters a deeper connection and reinforces the trust you have in each other.

As you continue on your journey to forever, remember that trust is not a static element in your marriage. It is dynamic, evolving with every choice you make, and every challenge you face together. By nurturing transparency, forgiveness, honoring commitments, building trust with God, and practicing effective communication and empathy, you strengthen the pillar of trust upon which your marriage is built. This pillar will provide the stability and strength to weather any storm, and in turn, it will enable your love to grow deeper and your commitment to flourish.

3

Cultivating Compassion and Kindness

The Journey to Forever: A Christian Marriage Roadmap

In the heart of every Christian marriage, compassion and kindness serve as the tender soil from which love blossoms and thrives. These qualities, deeply rooted in Christian teachings, are the nurturing forces that sustain the bond between spouses and foster an atmosphere of love and unity. In this chapter, we explore the significance of cultivating compassion and kindness in your marriage.

3.1 The Essence of Compassion

"Finally, all of you, be like-minded, be sympathetic, love one another, be compassionate and humble." - 1 Peter 3:8

Compassion is the act of understanding and sharing in the emotions of your spouse. It is the empathy that allows you to walk in their shoes, to feel their joys and sorrows, and to provide support in times of need. Compassion is not a fleeting emotion but a continuous choice to be there for one another.

3.2 The Power of Kindness

"Be kind and compassionate to one another, forgiving each other, just as in Christ God forgave you." - Ephesians 4:32

Kindness is a deliberate choice to treat each other with grace and respect. It is the gentle touch that soothes the soul and the words that uplift and inspire. Just as Christ's kindness extends to us despite our imperfections, your kindness toward each other fosters a loving and harmonious atmosphere in your marriage.

3.3 Embracing Selflessness

"Do nothing out of selfish ambition or vain conceit. Rather, in humility, value others above yourselves." - Philippians 2:3

To cultivate compassion and kindness, one must practice selflessness. It is the ability to place your spouse's needs and desires above your own. Selflessness allows you to serve and support one another without expecting anything in return, creating a virtuous cycle of care and affection.

3.4 Forgiving as Christ Forgave

"Bearing with one another and, if one has a complaint against another, forgiving each other; as the Lord has forgiven you, so you also must forgive." - Colossians 3:13

Forgiveness is an integral aspect of compassion and kindness. It is the choice to let go of past wrongs and grievances, just as Christ forgave us. In forgiving your spouse, you extend grace and make room for growth and renewal in your relationship.

3.5 A Grateful Heart

"Give thanks in all circumstances; for this is the will of God in Christ Jesus for you." - 1 Thessalonians 5:18

Cultivating compassion and kindness is intertwined with gratitude. Expressing gratitude for your spouse and the blessings in your marriage creates an atmosphere of appreciation and love. A heart full of thankfulness is less likely to harbor resentment or unkindness.

3.6 Prayer and Reflection

"Continue steadfastly in prayer, being watchful in it with thanksgiving." - Colossians 4:2

In the hustle and bustle of life, it's essential to take time for prayer and reflection. Seek God's guidance, find strength in His word, and reflect on the compassion and kindness Christ extended to all. In doing so, you will find inspiration to cultivate these qualities in your marriage.

Cultivating compassion and kindness is an ongoing process that nurtures the love and unity in your Christian marriage. By embracing these qualities, you create an environment where love not only endures but flourishes. As you continue your journey to forever, remember that compassion and kindness are the hands that tend to the garden of your love, enabling it to grow deeper and more beautiful with each passing day.

4

Cherishing Unity and Oneness

The Journey to Forever: A Christian Marriage Roadmap

In a Christian marriage, unity and oneness are the strong bonds that hold two souls together as they journey through life as one. The idea of becoming one in the eyes of God is a cornerstone of Christian matrimony. In this chapter, we delve into the profound significance of cherishing unity and oneness in your marriage.

4.1 God's Design for Unity

"...and the two will become one flesh. So they are no longer two, but one flesh." - Mark 10:8

God's design for marriage is the union of two individuals into a single, harmonious entity. In this sacred covenant, you embark on a journey to become not only partners but one in spirit, intention, and purpose. Your unity reflects God's intention for love, support, and companionship in marriage.

4.2 A Partnership of Equals

"In the Lord, however, woman is not independent of man, nor is man independent of woman. For as woman came from man, so also man is born of woman. But everything comes from God." - 1 Corinthians 11:11-12

In unity, both spouses are equal partners. They complement and support each other, recognizing that they are interdependent. Neither is more important than the other, and both are cherished and celebrated for their unique strengths and qualities.

4.3 The Power of Agreement

"Again, truly I tell you that if two of you on earth agree about anything they ask for, it will be done for them by my Father in heaven." - Matthew 18:19

Unity in marriage empowers you to act in agreement, seeking God's will together. This collective effort in prayer and decision-making allows you to tap into the promises of heavenly support and guidance, reinforcing your unity and strengthening your bond.

4.4 Cherishing Differences

"For just as the body is one and has many members, and all the members of the body, though many, are one body, so it is with Christ." - 1 Corinthians 12:12

Unity does not imply uniformity. It celebrates the beauty of diversity within your marriage. Just as the body has many different parts, each with a unique role, your unity allows you to appreciate and cherish each other's differences while functioning as one cohesive whole.

4.5 Guarding Against Division

"I appeal to you, brothers, by the name of our Lord Jesus Christ, that all of you agree, and that there be no divisions among you, but that you be united in the same mind and the same judgment." - 1 Corinthians 1:10

Division can erode the unity of a marriage. Guard against conflicts that divide your partnership. Communication, mutual respect, and prayer are tools to mend division, preserving the unity that is at the core of your marriage.

4.6 United in Faith

"For you are all sons of God through faith in Christ Jesus." - Galatians 3:26

In a Christian marriage, faith is the glue that binds you together. It's the shared belief in Christ, the cornerstone of your unity. Your faith is a constant reminder of your commitment to follow God's path, united in your spiritual journey.

Cherishing unity and oneness is not just a concept; it is a way of life in a Christian marriage. Your journey to forever is a pilgrimage of two souls becoming one, supported by the divine love and purpose ordained by God. As you continue on this path, remember that unity is the strength that enables you to face all challenges together and celebrate every joy as a single, harmonious entity.

5

Nurturing Intimacy and Connection

The Journey to Forever: A Christian Marriage Roadmap

In the sanctuary of Christian marriage, intimacy and connection serve as the sacred garden where love, trust, compassion, and unity blossom. This chapter explores the profound significance of nurturing intimacy and connection in your marriage.

5.1 The Heart of Intimacy

"Love is patient, love is kind. It does not envy, it does not boast, it is not proud." - 1 Corinthians 13:4

Intimacy is a reflection of love in its purest form. It is the act of being known deeply, and yet loved unconditionally. In your Christian marriage, it is about sharing your most authentic selves, free from judgment or fear. As God loves you without condition, your love should encompass the same grace.

5.2 Emotional Intimacy

"Two are better than one because they have a good return for their labor: If either of them falls down, one can help the other up." - Ecclesiastes 4:9-10

Emotional intimacy is the foundation of a thriving marriage. It involves sharing your thoughts, fears, and dreams with your spouse. It is the bond that helps you weather life's storms together and celebrate its joys. In nurturing emotional intimacy, you create a safe space for vulnerability, trust, and growth.

5.3 Physical Intimacy

"The husband should fulfill his marital duty to his wife, and likewise the wife to her husband." - 1 Corinthians 7:3

Physical intimacy is an essential aspect of marriage, designed by God to bond spouses together. It's a means of expressing your love in a unique, sacred way. Cherish the gift of physical intimacy and approach it with love, respect, and consent, keeping God's design for it at its core.

5.4 Spiritual Intimacy

"Love the Lord your God with all your heart and with all your soul and with all your mind." - Matthew 22:37

Spiritual intimacy is the bond that connects you and your spouse to God. By nurturing your individual relationships with Him and coming together in worship, prayer, and spiritual exploration, you strengthen your connection as a couple and grow in faith together.

5.5 Keeping the Flame Alive

"Do not deprive each other except perhaps by mutual consent and for a time, so that you may devote yourselves to prayer. Then come together again so that Satan will not tempt you because of your lack of self-control." - 1 Corinthians 7:5

Maintaining intimacy is essential. Challenges may arise, but regular communication, open discussion, and mutual respect are keys to keeping the flame of intimacy alive. Do not neglect your physical and emotional connection, for it is the heartbeat of your Christian marriage.

5.6 The Role of Gratitude

"Give thanks in all circumstances; for this is the will of God in Christ Jesus for you." - 1 Thessalonians 5:18

A grateful heart fosters intimacy and connection. Express gratitude for the gift of your spouse and the blessings in your marriage. A heart full of thankfulness strengthens your bond and kindles the fires of intimacy.

Nurturing intimacy and connection in your Christian marriage is a beautiful and fulfilling journey. It is the space where the essence of your love is shared, deepened, and celebrated. As you continue on the path to forever, remember that intimacy and connection are not just experiences but profound gifts from God, providing warmth, depth, and strength to your relationship.

6

Sustaining Hope and Resilience

The Journey to Forever: A Christian Marriage Roadmap

In the tapestry of a Christian marriage, hope and resilience are the threads that weave through every challenge, trial, and triumph. This chapter explores the profound significance of sustaining hope and resilience in your marriage.

6.1 The Power of Hope

"Now faith is confidence in what we hope for and assurance about what we do not see." - Hebrews 11:1

Hope is the beacon that guides you through the darkest nights. It's the unwavering belief that, no matter the circumstances, God's love and purpose will prevail. In your Christian marriage, hope is the anchor that keeps you steady in the face of uncertainty.

6.2 The Resilience of Love

SUSTAINING HOPE AND RESILIENCE

"Love is patient, love is kind. It does not envy, it does not boast, it is not proud." - 1 Corinthians 13:4

Resilience is the ability to endure and adapt in the face of challenges. Love, as described in 1 Corinthians, encapsulates the spirit of resilience. It is patient and kind, enduring all hardships, and always persevering. Your love is the wellspring of resilience in your marriage.

6.3 Weathering the Storms

"When you pass through the waters, I will be with you; and when you pass through the rivers, they will not sweep over you." - Isaiah 43:2

Every marriage faces storms, whether they be in the form of financial struggles, health crises, or relational challenges. The promise of God's presence in Isaiah 43:2 is a reminder that no matter the challenges you face, you will not be swept away if you rely on His guidance.

6.4 Learning from Trials

"Not only so, but we also glory in our sufferings because we know that suffering produces perseverance; perseverance, character; and character, hope." - Romans 5:3-4

Trials in your marriage have a purpose. They build your character, cultivate perseverance, and ultimately strengthen the hope that binds you together. Embrace these trials as opportunities for growth and transformation.

6.5 The Role of Prayer

"Do not be anxious about anything, but in every situation, by prayer and petition, with thanksgiving, present your requests to God." - Philippians 4:6

In sustaining hope and resilience, prayer is your most powerful tool. Share your concerns, fears, and hopes with God, and seek His guidance in navigating the challenges that come your way. In prayer, you find the strength to face any obstacle.

6.6 Encouraging Each Other

"And let us consider how we may spur one another on toward love and good deeds." - Hebrews 10:24

Encouraging and supporting one another is essential in maintaining hope and resilience. In a Christian marriage, you are each other's greatest allies and confidants. Your love and support are powerful motivators to face life's challenges with determination and grace.

Sustaining hope and resilience in your Christian marriage is not just about surviving the storms but thriving through them. It's about understanding that trials are opportunities for growth and that God's love and presence will see you through any adversity. As you continue on your journey to forever, remember that hope and resilience are the foundation upon which you build a love that endures and strengthens with each passing day.

7

Embracing Change and Growth

The Journey to Forever: A Christian Marriage Roadmap

Change is the rhythm of life, and growth is its melody. In your Christian marriage, these two are the tunes that will accompany you as you journey to forever. This chapter explores the profound significance of embracing change and nurturing growth within your partnership.

7.1 Embracing Change

"To everything there is a season, a time for every purpose under heaven." - Ecclesiastes 3:1

Change is inevitable. Your lives, individually and together, will evolve. Just as seasons shift and cycles turn, so will your marriage. Embracing change means being open to the shifts in your relationship, expectations, and dreams. With faith, you can weather the changes that come your way.

7.2 Adapting to Life's Twists

"Many are the plans in a person's heart, but it is the Lord's purpose that prevails." - Proverbs 19:21

In your Christian marriage, adaptability is a vital skill. It means being flexible and open to the unexpected twists and turns of life. Remember that God's plan is greater than any you may have. Embracing change requires the wisdom to understand that the path you didn't plan may lead to the greatest blessings.

7.3 Encouraging Individual Growth

"For I know the plans I have for you, declares the Lord, plans for welfare and not for evil, to give you a future and a hope." - Jeremiah 29:11

Individual growth is a crucial element in sustaining a thriving marriage. Each of you has your own unique journey in life. Encourage one another to pursue personal goals, dreams, and passions. Support and celebrate each other's successes, trusting that God has a plan for each of you.

7.4 Nurturing Shared Growth

"As iron sharpens iron, so one person sharpens another." - Proverbs 27:17

While individual growth is important, shared growth is equally vital in a Christian marriage. This includes developing common goals, dreams, and plans for the future. As you grow together, you strengthen your unity and deepen your bond.

7.5 The Role of Communication

"Let your conversation be always full of grace, seasoned with salt, so that you may know how to answer everyone." - Colossians 4:6

Effective communication is key in embracing change and nurturing growth. It allows you to share your evolving thoughts, desires, and aspirations. Listening with empathy and offering support is crucial in this process.

7.6 The Power of Gratitude

"Give thanks in all circumstances; for this is the will of God in Christ Jesus for you." - 1 Thessalonians 5:18

Gratitude is a cornerstone of embracing change and nurturing growth. It helps you appreciate the beauty of your journey, even when it takes unexpected turns. A heart full of thankfulness fosters a positive perspective and encourages a spirit of hope and joy.

Embracing change and nurturing growth is an essential aspect of your Christian marriage. It signifies your willingness to adapt to the ever-evolving journey of life and love. As you continue on the path to forever, remember that change is not an obstacle but an opportunity, and growth is not a destination but a lifelong journey that you undertake together.

8

Fostering Family and Legacy

The Journey to Forever: A Christian Marriage Roadmap

In the heart of every Christian marriage lies the desire to build a family and leave a legacy rooted in love, faith, and shared values. This chapter explores the profound significance of fostering family and legacy within your partnership.

8.1 God's Design for Family

"Children are a heritage from the Lord, offspring a reward from him." - Psalm 127:3

Family is a gift from God, and it is through family that you have the opportunity to leave a lasting legacy. The desire to build a family, guided by the principles of love and faith, is a calling that echoes the divine design of creation.

8.2 The Building Blocks of Family

"Fathers, do not provoke your children to anger, but bring them up in the discipline and instruction of the Lord." - Ephesians 6:4

Family is constructed upon the values you impart to your children. Fostering a nurturing and godly environment means instilling discipline, instruction, and love in their lives. Your actions and guidance shape the foundation upon which your family's legacy is built.

8.3 The Importance of Unity

"Behold, how good and pleasant it is when brothers dwell in unity!" - Psalm 133:1

Unity within your family is essential. A united front demonstrates the love and support you provide for your children. Your family, guided by shared values and principles, serves as a haven in which your children can grow, learn, and flourish.

8.4 Passing Down Faith

"Train up a child in the way he should go; even when he is old he will not depart from it." - Proverbs 22:6

Fostering a family and legacy means passing down the gift of faith. It is your responsibility to teach your children about God's love, grace, and the Christian values that have guided your own journey. Faith is the cornerstone upon which your legacy will stand.

8.5 Leading by Example

"Follow my example, as I follow the example of Christ." - 1 Corinthians 11:1

Your actions speak volumes to your children. Leading by example means living out the values you seek to instill in them. Your own faith and commitment to your Christian marriage will set a powerful example for your children to follow.

8.6 Celebrating Traditions and Memories

"Then these days will be remembered and observed throughout every generation, every family, every province, and every city; and these days of Purim will never cease among the Jews, and the memory of them will never die out among their descendants." - Esther 9:28

Traditions and shared memories are the threads that weave together a family's legacy. Celebrate special moments, holidays, and milestones as a family. These traditions will create cherished memories and bonds that will carry on for generations.

Fostering family and legacy within your Christian marriage is a sacred calling and a profound responsibility. As you continue on your journey to forever, remember that your family is the living testament to your love, faith, and values. The legacy you leave behind will echo your commitment to God, each other, and the generations that follow in your footsteps.

9

Sustaining Gratitude and Joy

The Journey to Forever: A Christian Marriage Roadmap

In the tapestry of a Christian marriage, gratitude and joy are the vibrant threads that infuse life with love, positivity, and appreciation. This chapter delves into the profound significance of sustaining gratitude and joy in your marriage.

9.1 Gratitude as a Daily Practice

"Give thanks to the Lord, for he is good; his love endures forever." - 1 Chronicles 16:34

Gratitude is not merely an occasional sentiment; it's a daily practice in a Christian marriage. Begin each day by thanking God for your spouse, your love, and the life you share together. A heart filled with gratitude is a heart open to love and joy.

9.2 The Power of Counting Blessings

"Let the peace of Christ rule in your hearts since as members of one body you were called to peace. And be thankful." - Colossians 3:15

Counting your blessings helps you recognize the beauty and abundance in your life. In moments of challenge or doubt, remember the countless ways in which God has blessed your marriage. It brings peace and reminds you of God's presence in your journey.

9.3 Finding Joy in the Little Things

"May the God of hope fill you with all joy and peace as you trust in him so that you may overflow with hope by the power of the Holy Spirit." - Romans 15:13

Joy can be found in the smallest of moments. A shared smile, a heartfelt laugh, or a simple gesture can bring immeasurable joy. In your marriage, seek out these moments and cherish them as gifts from God.

9.4 Celebrating Milestones

"A joyful heart is good medicine, but a crushed spirit dries up the bones." - Proverbs 17:22

Life is filled with milestones, both big and small. Celebrate these moments with joy and gratitude. Whether it's an anniversary, a birthday, or an achievement, these celebrations strengthen the bonds of love and remind you of God's grace in your marriage.

9.5 Overcoming Challenges with a Grateful Heart

"Consider it pure joy, my brothers and sisters, whenever you face trials of many kinds because you know that the testing of your faith produces perseverance." - James 1:2-3

Challenges are part of life, and they, too, can be met with gratitude and joy. They are opportunities for growth, perseverance, and deepening your faith. A grateful heart can find joy even in the midst of adversity.

9.6 Spreading Joy to Others

"A cheerful heart is good medicine, but a crushed spirit dries up the bones." - Proverbs 17:22

Your joy and gratitude have the power to spread to those around you. As a couple, you can be a source of encouragement, inspiration, and joy for your family and community. Your marriage is a reflection of God's love and can be a beacon of light in the lives of others.

Sustaining gratitude and joy in your Christian marriage is not just a personal endeavor; it's a witness to God's grace and an offering of love to the world. As you continue on the path to forever, remember that a heart filled with gratitude and joy not only enriches your relationship but also radiates God's love to all those you encounter on your journey.

10

Leaving a Legacy of Love

The Journey to Forever: A Christian Marriage Roadmap

In the final chapter of this Christian marriage roadmap, we explore the concept of leaving a legacy of love. Your journey to forever has been a remarkable adventure, and now it's time to reflect on how you can leave a lasting imprint of love, faith, and values for generations to come.

10.1 The Legacy of Love

"A new command I give you: Love one another. As I have loved you, so you must love one another." - John 13:34

Love is the cornerstone of your legacy. The love you have shared with your spouse, your children, and your community is a testament to the love of Christ. It's a legacy that continues to grow, branch out, and inspire others to love as you have loved.

10.2 Passing Down Values

"Start children off on the way they should go, and even when they are old they will not turn from it." - Proverbs 22:6

Your Christian values are a precious legacy to pass on. By teaching your children about faith, compassion, kindness, and the importance of living according to God's word, you leave a legacy that guides them throughout their lives.

10.3 The Power of Stories

"I will tell of the kindnesses of the Lord, the deeds for which he is to be praised, according to all the Lord has done for us." - Isaiah 63:7

Sharing your journey, your challenges, and your triumphs with your family and friends creates a legacy of wisdom and inspiration. Your stories become a part of their history, offering lessons, encouragement, and a sense of belonging.

10.4 Fostering a Welcoming Home

"Each of you should use whatever gift you have received to serve others, as faithful stewards of God's grace in its various forms." - 1 Peter 4:10

Your home can be a place of refuge and love for your family and friends. By opening your doors and hearts to those in need, you create a legacy of hospitality, generosity, and service. Your home is a reflection of God's love and grace.

10.5 Leading by Example

"Whoever claims to live in him must live as Jesus did." - 1 John 2:6

Leading by example means living a life that aligns with your Christian values.

It means showing your family and community what it means to love, serve, and follow Christ. Your actions become the most powerful testament to your faith and love.

10.6 A Message of Hope

"For I know the plans I have for you, declares the Lord, plans for welfare and not for evil, to give you a future and a hope." - Jeremiah 29:11

Your legacy is not just a reflection of the past; it's a message of hope for the future. It's a reminder to your children and the generations that follow that with faith and love, there is always hope for a better future. Your legacy is a continuation of God's plan.

Leaving a legacy of love in your Christian marriage is the final, beautiful act in your journey to forever. It's a testament to the love, faith, and values that have guided your relationship, and it's a gift that keeps on giving, inspiring others to follow in your footsteps. As you continue on your path, remember that your legacy is not just the result of your love; it's the embodiment of God's love working through you and radiating out into the world.

11

Celebrating the Journey

The Journey to Forever: A Christian Marriage Roadmap

As we come to the final chapter of this Christian marriage roadmap, it's time to reflect on the journey you've embarked upon and to celebrate the love, faith, and commitment that have sustained your union. This chapter is a celebration of your journey to forever, acknowledging the challenges you've overcome and the joys you've shared.

11.1 A Reflection on Your Journey

"Give thanks to the Lord, for he is good; his love endures forever." - Psalm 106:1

Take a moment to reflect on the path you've traveled together. Remember the highs and the lows, the victories and the setbacks. Give thanks to the Lord for His guidance and grace throughout your journey.

11.2 The Joy of Togetherness

"Though one may be overpowered, two can defend themselves. A cord of three strands is not quickly broken." - Ecclesiastes 4:12

Celebrate the power of togetherness in your Christian marriage. Your love and faith have fortified your bond, making it unbreakable. Rejoice in the knowledge that you've faced life's challenges hand in hand, growing stronger as a couple.

11.3 Cherishing Your Love

"Many waters cannot quench love; rivers cannot sweep it away." - Song of Solomon 8:7

Your love is a beacon that cannot be extinguished. It's a force that has withstood the trials and tribulations of life, emerging even more resilient and radiant. Celebrate the depth and endurance of your love.

11.4 Gratitude for God's Guidance

"Trust in the Lord with all your heart and lean not on your own understanding; in all your ways submit to him, and he will make your paths straight." - Proverbs 3:5-6

Express your gratitude for God's unwavering guidance. His wisdom has illuminated your path, allowing you to navigate the journey with faith and hope. Celebrate the trust you've placed in Him and the straight paths He has made for you.

11.5 Sharing Your Journey

"Carry each other's burdens, and in this way, you will fulfill the law of Christ." - Galatians 6:2

Acknowledge the importance of sharing your journey with your spouse. By carrying each other's burdens, you've lightened the load and enriched your connection. Celebrate the love and support you've provided for one another.

11.6 A Message of Hope for Others

"Each of you should use whatever gift you have received to serve others, as faithful stewards of God's grace in its various forms." - 1 Peter 4:10

Celebrate the role you play as stewards of God's grace. Your journey serves as a message of hope and inspiration for others. It's a testament to the transformative power of love and faith in the context of Christian marriage.

11.7 A Vision for the Future

"Hope does not disappoint us because God's love has been poured into our hearts." - Romans 5:5

Look to the future with hope and excitement. Your journey continues, and with God's love poured into your hearts, there is no limit to the love, faith, and joy that you can create together. Celebrate the uncharted paths that lie ahead.

As you celebrate the journey to forever in your Christian marriage, remember that it's not just the destination that matters, but the path you've traveled. The challenges you've overcome, the love you've shared, and the faith that has sustained you are all reasons for celebration. Your journey is a testament to the enduring power of love and faith, and it's a source of inspiration for those who follow in your footsteps.

12

The Everlasting Covenant

The Journey to Forever: A Christian Marriage Roadmap

As we conclude this Christian marriage roadmap, we arrive at the pinnacle of your journey: the everlasting covenant. This chapter is a celebration of the sacred and unbreakable bond you've formed through your love, faith, and commitment to one another and to God.

12.1 The Everlasting Promise

"I will establish my covenant as an everlasting covenant between me and you and your descendants after you for the generations to come, to be your God and the God of your descendants after you." - Genesis 17:7

In your Christian marriage, you've made a promise not only to each other but to God. This covenant is a sacred commitment to love, honor, and support one another for a lifetime. It is the foundation upon which your journey to forever is built.

12.2 The Unwavering Commitment

"Though one may be overpowered, two can defend themselves. A cord of three strands is not quickly broken." - Ecclesiastes 4:12

Your commitment is like a cord of three strands, with you, your spouse, and God woven together. This unbreakable bond is a testament to the strength of your love and faith. It's a commitment that endures through all the seasons of life.

12.3 The Blessings of Unity

"How good and pleasant it is when God's people live together in unity!" - Psalm 133:1

Your unity as a couple is a source of blessings not only for yourselves but for your family and community. Your marriage reflects God's design for love and companionship, inspiring others to seek unity and harmony in their own lives.

12.4 The Gift of Love

"Love is patient, love is kind. It does not envy, it does not boast, it is not proud." - 1 Corinthians 13:4

Your love, as described in 1 Corinthians, is a precious gift. It's patient and kind, enduring all hardships and rejoicing in truth. This love is a reflection of God's love for you, and it's a gift that keeps on giving.

12.5 The Journey Continues

"For I know the plans I have for you, declares the Lord, plans for welfare and not for evil, to give you a future and a hope." - Jeremiah 29:11

The journey to forever never truly ends. It's a continuation of God's plan for your lives, filled with hope, love, and faith. As you navigate the path ahead, trust in God's guidance, and remember that He has plans for your welfare and a bright future.

12.6 A Covenant Renewed

"As for me and my household, we will serve the Lord." - Joshua 24:15

Renew your commitment to your Christian marriage and to God. Your journey continues with each passing day, each challenge you overcome, and each moment of joy you share. As a couple, declare your intention to serve the Lord and to uphold the covenant you've made, ensuring that your love will endure forever.

The everlasting covenant of your Christian marriage is a testament to the strength of your love and the guidance of God. As you continue your journey to forever, remember that this covenant is the unbreakable bond that will see you through all the seasons of life. It's a promise to love, honor, and cherish one another, come what may, and to serve the Lord as a united and faithful couple.

Book Summary: "The Journey to Forever: A Christian Marriage Roadmap"

"The Journey to Forever: A Christian Marriage Roadmap" is a comprehensive guide that explores the sacred and profound journey of Christian marriage. This book takes readers on a voyage through the various stages of marriage, offering valuable insights, wisdom, and guidance to help couples build a love that lasts a lifetime.

The book is divided into twelve chapters, each addressing a crucial aspect of Christian marriage, from the foundational principles of love and commitment to the importance of nurturing intimacy, sustaining hope and resilience, and fostering family and legacy. Throughout these chapters, readers will discover the significance of love, faith, and unity in marriage, guided by biblical verses and Christian values.

Each chapter delves into the theological and practical elements of Christian marriage, offering thought-provoking reflections, personal stories, and actionable advice. The authors emphasize the importance of faith, unity, and shared values in building a strong marital foundation. They also highlight the role of gratitude, joy, and hope in creating a lasting, loving partnership.

"The Journey to Forever" invites couples to reflect on their own marriage, encouraging them to deepen their love, embrace challenges, and leave a legacy of faith and love. The authors emphasize the unbreakable bond of the everlasting covenant that ties couples together and to God, reassuring readers that their journey continues with hope and divine guidance.

This book is not only a practical guide for couples navigating the challenges and joys of marriage but also a source of inspiration for those seeking to strengthen their relationships in accordance with Christian values. "The Journey to Forever" offers a powerful message that love, faith, and unity can endure through all of life's seasons, making it an invaluable resource for couples committed to a lifelong journey together.

www.ingramcontent.com/pod-product-compliance
Lightning Source LLC
LaVergne TN
LVHW020457080526
838202LV00057B/6001